TO: _____

FROM: _____

W9-AHC-862

Then They Do

TRACE ADKINS

JIM COLLINS AND SUNNY RUSS

RUTLEDGE HILL PRESS™ | NASHVILLE, TENNESSEE
A DIVISION OF THOMAS NELSON, INC. | WWW.THOMASNELSON.COM

Published by Rutledge Hill Press, a Division of Thomas Nelson, Inc.,
P.O. Box 141000, Nashville, Tennessee, 37214.

Design by Jackson Design: Design and Art Direction by Buddy Jackson and
Linda Bourdeaux • Nashville, TN • www.bjacksondesign.com

Photography: Getty Images

1-4016-0130-8

Printed in the United States of America
03 04 05 06 07—5 4 3 2 1

ACKNOWLEDGMENTS

WE WOULD LIKE TO THANK THE FOLLOWING PEOPLE FOR
THE USE OF THEIR STORIES IN THIS BOOK.

TERESA MOORE

CATHY JACKSON

MATT RANKIN

CORI PETERS

JULIE C. DOYLE

ARLENE MERRICK

JENNIFER S. TURNER

SALLY ANN SPRY

DOREEN K. ADAMS

AMY PALMER

OLA D. METTS

GORDON GAY

SHAWNEE RYAN

CONNIE POWELL

BO SEBASTIAN

THEN THEY DO

In the early rush of morning | Trying to get the kids to school | One's hanging on my shirttail | Another's locked up | In her room | And I'm yelling up the stairs | Stop worrying 'bout your hair | You look fine.

Then they're fightin' in the backseat | I'm playing referee | Now someone's gotta go | The moment that we leave | And everybody's late | I swear that I can't wait | Till they grow up.

Chorus: Then they do | And that's how it is | It's just quiet in the morning | Can't believe | How much you miss | All they do | And all they did | You want all the dreams | They dreamed of | To come true | Then they do.

Now the youngest is starting college | She'll be leavin' in the Fall | And Brianna's latest boyfriend | Called to ask if we could talk | And I got the impression | That he's about to pop the question any day.

I look over at their pictures | Sittin' in their frames | I see them as babies.

I guess that'll never change | You pray all their lives | That someday they will find happiness.

Chorus: Then they do | And that's how it is | It's just quiet in the morning | Can't believe | How much you miss | All they do | And all they did | You want all the dreams | They dreamed of | To come true | Then they do.

No more Monday PTA's | No carpools | Or soccer games | Your work is done | Now you've got time | That's all your own | You've been waitin' for so long | For those days to come.

Chorus: Then they do | And that's how it is | It's just quiet in the morning | Can't believe | How much you miss | All they do | And all they did | You want all the dreams | They dreamed of | To come true | Then they do.

— JIM COLLINS & SUNNY RUSS

WHEN I FIRST LISTENED TO THE SONG, "THEN THEY DO," I WAS, QUITE LITERALLY, STOPPED IN MY TRACKS— IT REALLY RANG TRUE TO HOW I FEEL AS A FATHER.

I am the married father of four daughters, so I'm the only male in a household of five girls (five girls!). My life as a father is sort of book-ended. On the one side, my oldest has just finished high school and is registering for college. And on the other end my youngest just enrolled in potty training. As I sit down to write this, I can mark the ages of my daughters in my head, marveling at the breadth of life and experience represented by the Adkins women: Tarah is eighteen and soon to be on her own for the first time. Sarah is fourteen and already talking about driving. Mackenzie, at just five years of age, is already very assertive and precocious. And Brianna, who at eighteen months, is very much the baby of the family. All of them are unique, beautiful, and headstrong.

I often find myself struck by the contrast between raising four girls versus growing up as one of three boys. My father never had to sit through a ballet recital or pick us up from cheerleading practice. It's a completely different set of challenges, and some days it feels like I'm speaking a different language. But in the end, it's all the same. It's all about being a father . . . about being there. I love my girls so much. Their happiness, their wants, their needs, always come before my own, and this is how it should be.

I thought when I first held my own son that there could be no greater love in me. But the love I feel for my two granddaughters transcends even that. In their tiny souls, I see my son and every moment of his life we shared together. A vast range of emotions surges through me, from sadness to pride.

I am sad because I fully realize now that I can never hold my son, my baby, like this ever again. But I am proud and happy, too, watching this grown man, my son, with daughters of his own!

How I wish I could hold him on my lap one more time or get to scold him for being so loud or rough!

I see now that my own new life is just beginning as I hold my son's girls. I know that one day he, too, will feel what I feel. ✠

Aiken, South Carolina

Big Shoes

My travel alarm clock was last year's Father's Day gift from my girls. Every time I pack a suitcase, kiss my wife and kids good-bye, and walk out the door, that clock goes with me. And it serves its purpose well. But more than just doing its job, it represents all the times I have had to go on the road. The time spent playing shows. Time spent in the studio. Time spent doing interviews. Each morning when I wake up in a strange city or find myself sitting up in the middle of the night in yet another hotel room, their little gift is with me, counting all the days, hours, and minutes until we are together again.

My children give me purpose. They make me want to be a better human being. From the moment they entered into the world they were under my care, protection, and guidance. It's a job that's never done, a responsibility that has no end. And it's one of the most joyous elements to life.

Today, more than ever, I always want to spend more time with them. Today I'll make more time because I know all too soon they'll be grown. As the song says, "You want the dreams they've dreamed of to come true—and then they do."

— TRACE ADKINS

MY COWRITER, JIM COLLINS, AND I WERE AT OPPOSITE ENDS OF OUR PARENTING JOURNEYS WHEN WE WROTE THIS SONG. It was the perfect combination as I am expecting my second child and his is grown. I've not made any mistakes with the new baby yet; I haven't forgotten to appreciate the small moments of each day . . . not just the beautiful spring days swinging in the park, but the impatient days too. Days when my four-year-old daughter blinks up at me with bright blue eyes, and says, "Mommy, are you mad at me?"

Did I sound mad? I didn't think I did. And as I gather her up in arms I am reminded, once again, to slow down, to take deep breaths, to breathe in the smell of her hair, and to listen to her delightful ramblings.

Our children are with us for such a short while—small voices in the park to loud voices on a football field to far away voices on the phone.

My prayer is that I won't wish or waste away any of my moments. And if there are days when I'd rather my children just leave me alone, I'll keep in mind that someday they will . . . and I know I'll wish we could start all over again.

— SUNNY RUSS

I'D LIKE TO START OFF BY SAYING "RAISING CHILDREN IS HARD." I learned that very quickly after my daughter was born. It reminds me of the joke that says, "the reason God made children so cute was so you wouldn't kill them."

There is so much about raising kids that you don't think about until they're here. There are diapers and baby formula and spit up on your shirt. Then it's teething, chicken pox, measles and the occasional temper tantrum at the grocery store for a particular toy they just have to have. And as they get older, especially for girls, there becomes a whole new set of problems. There are braces, training bras, makeup, and zits . . . and of course the always dreaded boyfriends.

I always said I couldn't wait till my daughter was grown . . . and now she is. My goodness, how time flies. In what seems like no time at all I've gone from taking training wheels off her bicycle to walking her down the aisle. That's right! Just last weekend my little girl got married. And when I saw her looking so beautiful in her wedding dress, I wished I had it to do all over again. That's what the song "Then They Do" means to me. It's about love unconditional. No matter how old she gets, she'll always be my baby, my greatest gift, and my greatest achievement.

I'm so proud to be a part of the song and now the book "Then They Do." I hope you will find something in the words and music that touches you. But most of all I hope you and your children's dreams will come true . . . Then They Do.

— JIM COLLINS

My Own Work of Art

At six months into the pregnancy of my second child, I found out that my baby had Down's syndrome. I had one fourteen-year-old boy who was fairly normal, except for typical teenage hormones. I had no idea what to expect from this forthcoming birth. I only knew that for whatever reason, God was taking this artist and sculptor on a journey far from her normal path.

When Jonah first looked up at me, I saw that I had no idea where to begin. Although a mild case, the doctors prepared me for the challenges to come. I realized early on that Jonah was going to be a lifetime commitment. This scared me to death.

I began to notice that Jonah was developing more slowly than other children. He began walking later and talking later, and he had a tendency to mimic me—my words and actions. Suddenly everything I did and everything I said became conscious doing—conscientious living. I had to represent right and good constantly, if I wanted my son—well, both of my sons—to be shaped with those same attributes. I've been forming and shaping lumps of clay and rock into beautiful pieces of art for the past fifteen years, but my children are the most

Goshen, Indiana

precious lumps of clay which God has given me to shape and model into beautiful works of art.

I've never really understood how a parent shapes a child until the day of Jonah's graduation from his High School, when I knew that, indeed, I had fashioned my child into a fine piece of humanity. He was chosen to represent his class by giving a short speech to the entire student body. He was so nervous. His teacher had helped him recite it into a tape recorder so he could practice it over and over again before the big night. For weeks he practiced faithfully, every night.

The evening of the graduation, I think I was more nervous than Jonah was. I couldn't imagine my son helping craft a speech, let alone reciting one to the entire student body. His first sentence and his last sentence that he spoke said it all: "My momma can look at a stone and make it into a face or a horse. . . . My momma looked at me and made me into a good student and the best son ever!" When Jonah smiled at the audience and laughed, I felt for the first time in my life that I truly was a sculptor, not of inanimate objects, but of two beautiful children. ✶

THE WILLOW TREE

Timothy was five when he began climbing the huge willow tree in our front yard. The branches were thick and gnarled. About every foot or so, the limbs unfolded into vicious wishbone V's that could trap a kid his size and hold him in their grip until he smothered to death. That was my fear.

Timothy is my oldest son, so I tended to cut him some slack. But every day I had to tell him to get out of that tree. He never listened. It was as if that tree had a voice louder and much more cunning than his own mother's. The temptation was greater than a five year old could withstand.

One summer day, as I was carrying groceries into the house, Timothy ran from my side and jumped up into the tree—right in front of me. This time, I bit my lip. I shook my head and proceeded into the house, where I began unloading groceries.

Holland, Michigan

Five minutes passed, and I heard nothing from Timothy, which was unusual. I stacked some canned goods in the pantry. Ten minutes, no Timothy. My heart started to pound. I threw the ground beef to the counter top and ran out front. There was Timothy stuck between two large branches about two feet above me, hanging by his knee like a wounded trapeze artist.

He didn't cry. He didn't shout. As I supported his bottom, he grunted with great wisdom: "This is the worst thing that's ever happened to me!" I agreed. It took four grown men, two policemen, and two firemen using the jaws of life to get that poor child out of the willow!

When Timothy was safe, standing under my protective wing again, one of the policemen asked him, "Well, son, what do you think? You ever gonna climb that tree again?"

Timothy gave him a quizzical grin, his eye brows crunched in the center. "Well, not that part!" ✭

CHECKING UP

When my son, Jason, was four, I became pregnant again. Daycare became a necessity a few days a week so that I could get things done around the house and rest. Just a half day was all I needed alone, then I'd pick up Jason. We'd spend the rest of the day together. He never seemed to mind daycare. He actually enjoyed playing with the other children.

One day I dropped him off and hustled to the grocery store and the bank. When I got back home, the phone was ringing. It was Jason. He told me he was calling to check on me. When I heard the words come out of his little mouth, I started to cry. How sweet! Every day I'd agonize about my little man hurting himself or getting into some kind of a jam. Now here he was worried about his mom.

I went to pick him up, and the ladies at the daycare all wore big smiles. "He asked to borrow the phone," the supervisor said. "You've got one wonderful caregiver!"

Jason is twenty now and in the U.S. Navy. I am as proud of him now as I was that day fifteen years ago. ✪

Rancho Palos Verdes, California

First Day of School

I wrote the following entry in my daughter Bea's scrapbook on her first day of school:

Today was your first day at kindergarten. We were both ready and even anxious for this day to arrive. I packed all your lunch favorites, a bologna and mustard sandwich cut into squares, a pack of cheese and peanut butter crackers, and chocolate milk. I even made Rice Krispy treats after you went to bed as an added surprise.

Your backpack had all the required supplies tucked inside. You wore the clothes you had laid out the night before. Yes, we were ready . . . but not quite prepared. At least, I wasn't. Not prepared for the onslaught of feelings that would overcome me as I left you in Miss Ellen's care!

I missed you and worried that I hadn't prepared you well enough for this day. Would you know how to behave or even how to open the flip top of your drink container? I wondered and worried all day while I was with your brother.

Franklin, Tennessee

Finally, we came to pick you up. I left Andrew in his car seat and walked slowly to meet you. Miss Ellen had her hands on your shoulders. Your face lit up as you called out, "Mommy!" It seemed in one same, excited breath, you shared with me about your gingerbread man hunt adventure and how you got to shake the maracas in music and how you ate lunch in the big room.

I could see in your joyous excitement that we had prepared well enough, that your behavior would naturally follow your exuberance, and that you must have handled your drink container just fine.

Thank you for putting to rest all my fears in those few brief and happy moments. You reminded me well that life is not a dress rehearsal. Carpe Diem, Beatrice Rose! ✦

GROWING SLOWLY

For eighty-four days, starting in December 1998, I spent every moment begging my son to grow. He was born prematurely, sixteen weeks early, weighing only one pound, six ounces. When I was finally allowed to hold him, I drew him close and pressed my nose against his tiny body, appreciating every breath, every miniscule movement, every gurgle.

He grew slowly, like that twig I'd planted in the front yard ten years earlier. It's finally a small tree.

My son is a rambunctious four year old now. When I see him jumping, hopping, and bringing me presents from goodness knows where . . . I remember him being the size of my palm.

Then I realize, "yes, they do grow." ✶

Mount Laurel, New Jersey

Secret Time Capsule

I worked in a dense group of pines in my backyard, cleaning up broken limbs from last winter's heavy snow. As I raked under one particular tree, I remembered my daughter playing there. Daddy's little girl, Lisa had managed her own private clubhouse there under branches so long that they bent all the way to the ground.

As I continued to rake, I made a miraculous discovery. A rich layer of pine needles had accumulated over the last fifteen years. This layer, now turning to compost, concealed wonderful secrets. As I began to rake away the years, I opened a time capsule.

First, I found little empty applesauce containers. Oh, this is where Lisa went to eat dessert after dinner. Then a strange green rectangular object appeared, dense with moisture. I read the words *The Colossal Book of Dinosaurs*. The pages were stuck together and slowly returning to the earth with the rest of the mulch.

Bainbridge, New York

Next a shiny object caught my eye. It was the spoon that Lisa must have used to dine on her private dessert. Little Lisa always had a habit of borrowing things and never returning them. This time, I'm glad. The little spoon is now one of a kind.

My daughter is grown up now. Some of the time, we don't get along very well. I am going to polish this spoon, though, and keep it in a special place so that I don't forget that things weren't always this way. ★

Big Enough to Walk

From the beginning of my third pregnancy, I complained about what a hard time I had carrying Sean. The doctors almost had to cut him out of me; he was so huge—ten pounds, six ounces. Once he was born, I found myself saying to him, "I can't wait until you learn to walk on your own. You are much too heavy for Mommy to carry."

Before I knew it, of course, I had to chase him around the room to catch him.

Now he is three and a half and still bigger than any kid his age. Now he's even harder to carry. At night, when he curls up in my lap, though, I run my fingers through his blond curls and watch him fall asleep. I guess asking God to stop the clock at this point is futile.

I asked my child to walk. Now I hope he never walks too far away! ✭

Fairfax, Virginia

ONLY YESTERDAY

I kept the first tooth she ever lost. After her first haircut, I saved a blond curl. At seven years old, she put a sticky note on the fridge that said, "Mommy, when I grow up, I promise that you can come and live with me, even if my husband doesn't like it. Too bad!" I salvaged that too.

Time scurried by. I realized that—in the blink of an eye—the baby girl taking her first bath in the kitchen sink turned into the five year old in pigtails clutching for my hand, scared to go to her first day of kindergarten. I suddenly found myself hanging on to just about everything she made and touched.

Then, without warning, she was ten, asking me for the third time, "Why can't you just drop me off at the skating rink with my friends without going in? I'll be okay. You never let me do anything!"

Hohenwald, Tennessee

Halfway through raising her, I realized that it felt like only yesterday when God had given me this incredible child to love and nurture. Every day, every hour, every moment is so precious.

Now she's a young woman, growing another inch taller, needing her father and me a little less each day. The pictures she drew for us are now like frames of the past I keep going back to, reliving her life every time I look at them. Because of what I have saved over the past eighteen years, I'll never forget one moment, not one instant, of this cherished gift—my baby girl. ✸

TRANSCENDING LOVE

Momma's Fried Bacon

One day I put on a pair of my friend's shoes to check the afternoon mail. Rick's feet were much larger than mine, so I tripped and flopped all the way down the street and back up the front steps, complaining under my breath the entire time.

My son stood at the door laughing at me. Obviously, he'd heard me mutter what I'd hoped he hadn't. "Those aren't Rick's shoes, Momma," he said. "They're mine!"

I looked up at him and immediately started to cry. Just yesterday, it seemed I had bought him little bitty Batman shoes at the K-Mart.

He hugged me and smiled. "Don't worry, Mom. I never once could fit into your shoes. Even when my feet were small." ✱

Trace Adkins

My husband is in the air force. Our family moved around a great deal, which was good for my three daughters, each of them two years apart. We lived in many places most kids never get to experience. After many years of travel, we received orders to move once again. This time, however, my oldest daughter had turned eighteen. She wanted to stay in Maryland and not move to Maine with the family.

My heart was broken. I couldn't leave my baby behind, alone. We had been together for eighteen years. She was my daughter, my friend, my firstborn.

The day we left, my daughter gave me one red rose. We cried together, the thorny stem holding all the pain and beauty of the moment. I didn't know whose heart was breaking more, mine or hers.

I put the rose on the dashboard of the car. It has been there for two years now. That's how long it has taken me to realize I cannot keep my children with me forever. Except in my heart. ✦

Akron, Ohio

ONE RED ROSE

In that moment, something changed forever between us. She saw in me that same love she had developed for a child she hadn't even seen yet.

She looked at me and told me she loved me and that she wanted her father. My husband was on the way to the hospital and made it in time to see our new granddaughter, Chloe, be brought into the room to be cleaned up by our son-in-law. My husband and I were so proud. When Michelle was wheeled into the room, Chloe was brought to her. But Michelle asked for her dad to have the honor of holding the baby first. That is a moment my husband will never forget. ★

My daughter, Michelle, is one of my best friends. She's twenty-two and a new mother. But growing up, she had a hard time being a middle child with one older brother and a younger one, both always seeming to get on her last nerve. A strong-willed child, Michelle became extremely independent, which caused plenty of feuding over the years. But I never lost sight of my belief that one day we would become friends. Just how close, I could never have predicted.

After getting married, Michelle informed my husband and me that she never wanted children. She became distraught when she discovered she was pregnant. But as the day approached that she would give birth, she was already becoming a wonderful mother. I could see compassion and love growing in her heart and eyes for her unborn child—that same love I had for her.

When Michelle went into labor, she seemed prepared and steady. But suddenly her child's heartbeat began to slow. The umbilical cord had wrapped around the baby's neck. The doctor had to do an emergency Caesarean. I held my child and told her I loved her and how proud I was of her.

Urbana, Ohio

The Middle Child

An empty chair once sat across from me. I gazed at it through eyes void of emotion, longing for it to be filled. But with what, I wasn't sure.

In that same chair now sits a wonderful spirit. He's full of imagination, ideas, feelings, and vast emotions that consume my every moment. His space is so full, bursting with exuberance. Always on the verge of fiery excitement, he shines bright and hot.

Once space existed in my life. Now I see only him—growing and learning, smiling, observing, absorbing, and giving back so much more than he knows.

Across from me sits my son. ★

Lebanon, Tennessee

AN EMPTY CHAIR

When Mom was alive, our family would play together in the yard, laughing, kids frolicking, parents loving and nurturing. Then suddenly, after her death, I noticed each of my sibling's lights began to dim, especially mine. Nothing I did seemed to help. After the first year, I remember I almost stopped talking completely. I would just sit and rock with Mary on the porch swing or watch television.

One day she brought a photo album out to the porch and handed it to me. When I turned the first page of the album, tears filled my eyes. In the middle of the page was a picture of my mother holding my baby sister's hand and mine. I pointed to my mother and said, "One day when Mom yelled at me, I told her I wished you were my mother." I shook my head and covered my teary eyes with my hand. "I never meant for her to die. Never." Mary hugged and held me.

Of course, I know now that my moment of anger didn't cause my mother's death. And I better understand God's perfect will for each of us. Mary is dying of complications caused by cancer. Last week, I put my arm around her as she laid her head on my shoulder. "God has a way of working everything out. Doesn't He?" I closed my eyes and remembered the day she moved in next door and how my whole life had changed. ✵

Wishes and needs merged the year my mother died.

Back in the time when fertility drugs were unheard of, my neighbor Mary and her husband, Emil, tried to have children. But God never seemed to answer their prayers. When they stopped trying, they moved into a small Pittsburgh suburb, next door to my family of six children. I was the youngest boy and became a son to them.

Sometimes in the evenings, I would sit for hours watching TV with them, like we belonged together. With my family having so many children, I figured my mom and dad wouldn't miss me much. I secretly wished with all my heart that I could be Mary and Emil's son.

In the spring of 1970, my mom died of complications from breast cancer, and my father was left to raise six kids by himself. My youngest sister was eight years old, and every child was two years older than the next, up to eighteen. My father ran the house like an army camp.

Hendersonville, Tennessee

Things Work Out

We could hear the band play from blocks away. As we reached the gate, we were met by the smell of hot dogs and hamburgers being cooked out on the grill. We climbed the bleachers to our seats and heard the sound of helmets crashing. Like jumping beans, cheerleaders' heads popped up and down at the front of the stands, shouting and encouraging each team member. But two names were missing from their lips.

I gazed at my husband with tears in my eyes. He knew with one look. We slowly got back in the car and drove home in silence.

Since that night, when our boys come home to visit, I don't much mind the smell of musty wet socks or finding petrified food in a bedroom corner. The house comes alive again, and I know all is well with my world. ✦

My husband and I raised two sons in small town Missouri. Both kids were active in four sports at a local Catholic school. Their opponents were always from no more than a fifty- to a hundred-mile radius. Though my husband and I both worked all day, we never missed one of our children's games.

Many nights we sat through games in terribly cold and rainy weather. When we got home, we often helped the boys with their homework and washed uniforms for the next day's game. That was our routine. We never once diverged from it.

When both kids graduated from high school and went on to college, my husband and I moved back home to Tennessee. On a Friday night when the weather began to turn crisp and the absence of our sons rose up like silence through our empty spare rooms, my husband said, "Hey, let's go to a high school football game!"

Franklin, Tennessee

Our Sons' Games

This summer I intend to watch my eldest son get married. As a mother, I raised my child to be independent and self-sufficient. Yet as the day comes when he leaves the nest, I find myself with mixed emotions. I am proud that he has become a man and is carving out a niche in life for a family and himself. I feel joy to see him happy and prosperous and healthy, but sorrow because I know I won't be there to watch the part that I've waited so long to see. It is as if I've nurtured a flower until it bloomed, then given it to another person to experience its beauty.

Parents spend eighteen-plus years protecting and loving their children, only to let them go to face the complexities of the world by themselves. I often find myself wishing my children could once again squeeze their six-foot frames back into the baby bodies I used to hold. Then I would watch them sleep through the night. I find myself slightly envious of my son's fiancée. She now gets to behold all that I have nurtured. Yet I have a new abundant joy that he has found love and someone to take care of him in my stead. What a bittersweet paradox. ✠

Portland, Michigan

My Son's Wedding

Daddy's favorite saying was: "When you grow up, you'll see." Well, we did, and now he's gone. Momma doesn't fry bacon anymore; the doctor says it's bad for her heart. My wife's a vegetarian and doesn't want to eat anything that once had a face. So I find myself at Elliston Diner sitting behind the grill listening to the bacon sizzle and taking a whiff of what Daddy smelled every morning of his life, just to be close to him.

The surgeon said there was metal in his lungs when he died. That's all I can remember now. When I close my eyes at night to think of him, I keep seeing small chunks of metal in his chest, bullets killing the best man I ever knew.

Yesterday, I sat at the same kitchen table I ate at every day of my childhood and told that nightmare to Momma, like a little boy. She laid her callused hands on my shoulders and said softly, "That's not a bad memory, Son. You're seeing what God wants you to see—your daddy's metals of honor!"

Momma didn't try to talk Daddy out of working in the foundry. She got up every morning at four o'clock so that when her husband of fifty years got up, she'd have bacon sizzling in the iron skillet. That was his favorite. Even after all those years, the smell of Momma's bacon frying always made Daddy want to get up in the morning. That's what he told me, and Daddy never lied.

Momma would do whatever it took to make Daddy's day better—to make all our days better. I don't ever remember her complaining. Not like me and my kids. After a long day in the office, I'm lucky to have remembered to buy milk for the morning cereal.

Daddy never stopped to wonder if he was hurting himself when he got up at four-thirty in the morning, five days a week, to go to the foundry to cut and fire metal into sheets and bars and firearms and whatever else he used to make. Daddy just knew that the foundry was the best paying job he'd ever had and that he'd wanted to send his three kids to college so they wouldn't have to work all day in the hundred-degree heat, as he had done.

Rancho Palos Verdes, California